Winter Moorings

ANDREW MCNEILLIE was born in North Wales and read English at Magdalen College, Oxford. Professor Emeritus at Exeter University, he is the founding editor of the magazine *Archipelago* and runs the Clutag Press. His poetry collections are *Nevermore* (Oxford Poets, 2000) and (from Carcanet) *Now, Then* (2002), *Slower* (2006) and *In Mortal Memory* (2010). *Losers Keepers*, an Agenda Edition, came out in 2011. His memoir *An Aran Keening* was published by Lilliput Press of Dublin in 2001.

T0099104

Also by Andrew McNeillie from Carcanet Press

Nevermore
Now, Then
Slower
In Mortal Memory

ANDREW McNEILLIE

Winter Moorings

CARCANET

First published in Great Britain in 2014 by
Carcanet Press Limited
Alliance House
Cross Street
Manchester M2 7AQ

www.carcanet.co.uk

A CIP catalogue record for this book is available from the British Library

ISBN 978 1 84777 248 0

The publisher acknowledges financial assistance from Arts Council England

Typeset by XL Publishing Services, Exmouth

for

my granddaughters

one day

with love

Acknowledgements

Some of these poems, or versions of them, have appeared in the following periodicals: *Agenda, New Walk, Oxford Magazine, PN Review, Poetry Wales, The Reader, Stand,* and *The Times Literary Supplement.* I am grateful to the editors concerned for their encouragement. Those others who have helped me in matters Irish know my gratitude for their help. I must thank Lawrence Woodcock for researches at the MoD. 'An English Airman's Death Recalled' grew from a project to annotate a reference in Tim Robinson's *Stones of Aran: Labyrinth* (1995). I am indebted to Iris Jones's *Wartime Littlehampton 1939 to 1945* (Littlehampton Local History Society Monograph, 2009). 'By Ferry, Foot, and Fate' was written for a *Festschrift* to Gordon Campbell. The epigraph to the collection is from Hopkins's poem 'The Bugler's First Communion', as to which, in a letter to Robert Bridges, he made the shocking confession: 'I am half inclined to hope the Hero of it may be killed in Afghanistan'. The soldier had been 'ordered to Moultan in the Punjaub' in September 1879.

Contents

Winter Moorings	11
Block: A Pulley Used in Running Rigging	12
Strong Lines	13
In the Wake of 'The Seafarer'	14
Words at Sea	17
Quay	18
Old Salt's Prayer	19
Trouvé: Rigg Bay	20
Machars: War & Peace	21
Laver Weed	23
Lafan	24
Island Hopping	25
By Ferry, Foot, and Fate	26
Lighthouse at Daybreak	34
Nightwatch	35
Critique of Judgement	36
On Looking into an Old Photograph	37
An English Airman's Death Recalled	38
'The sea goes all the way round the island'	46
On the Rocks Road	47
Cormorant	51
Port Sheánia Revisited	52
Harbour Inn	53
On Not Sailing to St Kilda	54
A Return of the Native	55
Blind	56
Requiem	57
Insomnia	60
Round About a Great Estate	61
Shore Leave	62
At the Landfill Site	63

Dress his days to a dextrous and starlight order.

Gerard Manley Hopkins

Winter Moorings

Anchored stern and bow, sea-logged to the gunwales:
So I have moored my mind for the winter ahead.
To be the more sea-worthy if all else fails
Come better weather and spring buries its dead.

Block: A Pulley Used in Running Rigging

I cannot put it down
Or knock it into shape
That world and time
Inside my head
Once no less real than
Today and as ordinary
As daylight delayed in a rhyme.

I'm beached by the flood
Caulking my dreams
Haunted by such men
As Johnnie Rogof, Jackie Craven
And other names
No one remembers
Hauling nets in all weathers.

I think of them and the pulley
To their hopes
That drew them to sea
And the stars' rigging
Taut as ever aloft
About their obscure lives
In that Welsh estuary.

Sufficient unto the day their lesson
Their names signed nowhere
As if written in water
And no thought spared
But to immerse in that world
An example to all and no one
Hauling fish into oblivion.

Strong Lines

Stars flicker to quick white heat and the tide
Glitters the shoals where waders pipe and scatter.
I shift in my sleep, as the waters break; and we ride
Towards youth and the mouth of September.

Sea-green again with fish in the estuary,
Their school passing through me into the Conwy.
I spend my days ashore making and mending
Memory into strong lines hooked on rhyming.

Too late to ask what that world means to me.
What could it say even if it knew my mind
By heart? We don't always see eye to eye.
There are more than enough losses to go round.

I cast my thought out as far as I can and wait.
The waters rush against me and I feel their weight.

In the Wake of 'The Seafarer'*

I can sing you a song   about myself
tell of travels   toil and trouble
terrors on tossed waves   suffered at sea
(*you know I can   I've sung it before*)
night-watch nightmares   at the prow
crashing by cliffs   feet frozen
frost-bound   sea-weary
at hunger's door   soul-cares seething
hot round my heart.   The lucky lubber
has no idea   how I spent winter
(*from worst of November*)   in paths of exile
wretched and sorrowful   hung with icicles
hit by hail   on ice-cold sea
lost to the world.   Nothing but roar of icy waves
met my ears.   Only the swan's song
gannet, gull   and curlew cry
gave me pleasure   in adversity
not laughter   and drink at the bar.
Storms beat   wind-torn cliffs
icy-feathered   kittiwake called
dewy-feathered   the erne yelled.
No caring kin   can comfort the desolate heart.
Truly the burgher   merry with wine
flushed with pride   has no idea
what painful wandering   I must bide
and how often weary   endure
in the paths of the sea.   (*So I fare now*
aboard my glossary   battered by cruces
in ink-black night   chasing more than
imitation   more than word for word
the seafarer's voice   calling out to me
Christian scribe-scribble   ditched in our wake.
No comfy reader   turning pages

---

* This version derives from the so-called 'Cill Mhuirbhigh Ms' attributed to the
Árainn Scribe (fl. 968–69) by Giraldus Cambrensis (?1146–?1220) who visited the
island during his Irish travels. Giraldus claimed to have discovered it 'caulking a
coracle', among other manuscripts whose thickness helped preserve it (BL Royal
MS 13 B VIII (a)). Ida Gordon dismissed the entire text as 'irredeemably corrupt'.
Little is known about the reputed scribe beyond a work on the age-old custom of
caoineadh.

knows what pains I take   and pangs suffer
at heart for her . . .)
                    . . . Night-shadows darkened.
Snow fell from North   frost
gripped ground   hail hammered earth
coldest grain.   My heart-thoughts –
troubled   now I must venture
on high streams   of tumultuous brine –
urge me always   far from here
seeking homeland   of foreign folk.
No one on earth's   so proud of spirit
so generous of gifts   so bold in youth
brave-of-deed   dear to his love
he does not fear   what doom fate
might deal him at sea.   He has no time to think
of harp-throb   or receiving of rings
pleasure in woman   nor worldly things
nor anything else   but waste of waters.
Who goes to sea   knows heart's care.
Groves blossom   burghs grow fair
meadows beautiful.   World quickens.
All things urge   spirit to embark
fare far   by flood-ways
though melancholy call   of summer's lord
the cuckoo bode   bitter heart-sorrow.
The lucky reader   blessed with comfort
does not know   suffering of those
who travel farthest   as far as they can go
in exile's ways.   So now my spirit flies
beyond my breast   over sea-flood
above whale-path   soars far and wide
to earth's four corners   – returning eager,
greedy for more   wildish destinies.*
The solitary flier's cry   urges irresistibly
the willing heart again   to take the whale-road.
And so for me   such heightened being
is hotter than   dead life on land.
I don't believe earth-wealth will   last forever.
Always without fail   one of three things
will render all uncertain   before the fatal hour:

---

* 'géosceaft ge-wild'. Among her numerous caveats, Gordon protests 'a total want of authority' here.

disease or age   or sword-hate
rip life from those   doomed to die.
For every one praise   of the living is best
of children hereafter   for good deeds
against enmity   daring deeds
against evil . . .

[*manuscript damaged . . .*]

Days all gone   of magnificence on earth.
There are no kings   no Caesars now
no gold-givers   without dirty money.
Now fallen all   that noble company.
Joys gone. Weaker men   wield world-power
thrive through trouble.   Glory fled.
Earth's nobility   grows old and sere
as shall every one   the world over.
Hoary-haired   old age comes on
faces grow pale.   We mourn old friends
sons of princes   given up to earth.
Body can't avail   when life leaves.
Can't swallow sweetness   nor feel pain
nor move hand   nor think with mind . . .

[*Here sea broke aboard   lines chopped through
kennings cracked.   He spoke his last word
on the walkie-talkie   down with both hands in the ink
unwished-for fate   for even your enemy . . .*]

Words at Sea

(after visiting Kettle's Yard)

They cannot be dabbed on to suggest
A swell with breaking waves or suspended
In bosomed arcs to float like clouds
On a canvas tugged by sunny wind

Or dispense with syntax and grammar
For those at-a-glance soundless effects
Of worlds half-drowned
In wintering rowboat style.

But oh how they stop the heart
On wreckage of bow or stern or washed-up lifebuoy
On Seamen's Mission's grievous memorial
On the lips of widows and their children.

Quay

I wait at the quay
And the quay waits.
There's many a thing more lasting than a person
I hear it say
At no great length.

Old Salt's Prayer

Pilot me, I pray, for ever more,
Adrift on the rock of the world
Chain paid out to rust's bitter end
And low tide in time's estuary drained
To its dregs, on pause the moon's full O
Buoyed agape up above,
As youth keeps its counsel
And reels the world to its door.

Late now, leaning in the jamb, head full
Of tides on a conch-shell coast at my ear
Glimmering far-cry and groundswell
Heart foot-tapping at mooring
Waiting still as if I know what for:
Pilot me, I pray, to sea once more.

Trouvé: Rigg Bay

I come here combing the sea's waste.
Indigestibles from the whale's belly:
Weed rich as dung, plastic husk, and the rest.
No knowing what might catch my eye
Or how it might set me thinking on beauty.
What shape fate gives to objects –
The sea being fate and fate a mystery
Questioning all laws that cause effects
To trace anew old lines on the map.

Now I stumble on a purple fish box
That declares where it comes from:
FOYLE FISHERMEN'S CO-OP
Greencastle, Ireland (No Unauthorised Use)
By some slick wave thrown up
At dead of night on the rocks
A catch of thin air, brim-full
To lift away elsewhere my afternoon.
I've heard tell it's a long way to Donegal.

Machars: War & Peace

i.m. Sam Rennie

Offshore beyond all tides but those of time,
Wreckage of a Mulberry Harbour
Scars the bay at low water, a living memory
To just about no one now. Its warning buoy
Seems, from where I am, to tilt at peace
In waves so short they're almost calm.
The world on the other side waxes and wanes,
Now promising rain with prophetic clarity,
Now keeping its word in a leaden barrage.

'The Lancasters taking off from Baldoon
Had seven minutes to make it over Cairnsmore,'
An ancient mariner tells me; and I look
Towards the invisible hill to get the measure of it,
To hear their din in my mind's ear.
My grandfather, born here a blacksmith's son,
Managed a production line that made them.
But I keep it to myself, a secret
Like that underground factory in England.

* * *

Set your self against the fullness of time.
Blind we go, and blind we see
What's new under the sun's brighter for rain.
Look anywhere and find beauty; landscape
-in-waiting, what you want it to be,
What you have brought with you to find:
Your heritage, unpreserved, lived day by day.
You have your own words for it
And need to hear them and share them.

Where steading names stand in for poetry
And resignation for happiness and sorrow,
The fortunes of dynasties as they rise and fall.
Now the old know only their own by sight,
The rest as strangers, native or in-comer,
As the future prevails like the incoming tide

Eager to erase and start again
In sure and certain hope of resurrection,
The circle unbroken by staying or leaving.

* * *

The wreck submerges again and
A cormorant bobs to the surface
To see which way the wind blows.
An ill wind for one blows another good.
I attend to my postcards. The tide falls.
By the time they arrive I'll be 'home'
And living for the next trip here again
Knowing each time might be the last time
Either for me or for someone.

Casualty of life's storm, or casualty of war:
Like Sam Rennie, riddled with shrapnel
Fighting through Italy. Feel the pieces.
Watch them move beneath the skin
From Monte Cassino to Kirkinner round.
He's waiting on the other side for someone now.
And tell me about the peace here
And just reward for service to one's country
And how a soul might mend.

Laver Weed

Once, he said, the local yield so poor,
They went to Achill Island via Rosslare
To harvest there instead. So far!
Only to find 'the sand was in'
And the weed no good.
But by morning the weed came clean.
Such a thing, it seemed a miracle of God.

A time and a place, I said.

Time was they'd drive from the Gower
North to Port Patrick near Stranraer
To work the Strand and the Knock.
The length and breadth of the coast,
Good shoreline folk still years before
Sent theirs by train, on trust to Swansea . . .
But time's not what it was any more.

Neither time nor place, I said.

Lafan

Already your long low tide draws me down
And your *trompe l'oeil* of sailing through sand
Runs my loss against those mussel banks
At the mouth between island and mainland.

At mere memory of your name I drown
And all that sails in me looks to the lifeboat
Whether *Tillie, Annie, Isabella* or *Lilly* –
And *What-Ho!* herself and the Menai Light.

From the saintly life of the headland I
Take spare comfort, grateful for small mercy,
The life of the head and the brain-cell
Flashing intermittent signal blindly.

Blind as in faith, on the sea of language,
The eighth sea with its own ports of call,
A mirror world in the world's image.
Here I come again by Lafan to make landfall.

Island Hopping

Today, bleaker herringbone without break,
No herring either; the weave making its haul
Out of woollen clouds and thin air,
Metaphysical-material, and fine downfall,
Haunting the heart of what it is to be solitary
In company, not arpeggio but archipelago,
Whether at bow or astern
For the furrow's sake or the coulter
Into night's black house where the peats burn
Until the morning's morning, smoulder
Like memories remembered by no one.

By Ferry, Foot, and Fate
A Tour in the Hebrides

It's one o'clock in the afternoon.
The ferry unloads to load again.
Clang of ramps and chorus of ignitions,
Roaring juggernauts in pole positions,
Hiss of air-brakes, flash of lights, and hazard-
Bleep cacophony ushers us aboard.
Crewmen haul ropes hand over hand
As since time immemorial. Land
Floats and drifts off. Ahead six hours of sea
Siren some to *mal-de-mer*, others into reverie,
Dreaming according to their repertoires.
But wherever we go for our pleasures –
The bars or decks, the depths, the TV's
Comforts or those uplifting distant skies
Where evening distils a purer light –
We'll all reach Barra before the night.

As for me, what do I bring in my bag?
Camcorder, notebook, an eye for a greylag . . .
Ash-stick in hand to beat off preconception.
No phone number for a mythical relation
Called MacNeill or anywhere but home
Where I now work at rhyme and half-rhyme
About an *arrière-pays*, an evermore,
Where sky and water wash ashore
And the symmetry of boats speaks of art
Within immensity, the sea: that keeps apart
While joining everything arpeggio
As here in the tattered archipelago.
For which please read a figure for my heart.
For which read too a figure for time's hurt
And every frayed and broken connection
Nothing can mend unless by invention.

The mind's near misses and far cries
Echo beyond time, and the seven seas.
All absence finds itself in presence first.
Departure heads towards now. Walk the worst
Out of yourself until you're rid of it,

Body and mind in step to a heartbeat.
I can't go on, I will go on, anti-clockwise
Round the island, east to west, the day's
Arc like a broken rainbow, yielding epiphanies
Sparely, as when I put to flight five geese
From a boggy field by the road and their
Beating wings hold me as if in mid-air
Yet firmly planted in the here-and-now
At something I would call peace although
The weather's din is deafening North Bay
And I have miles ahead at not half-way.
Which means I know my destination.
But how to make sense of devotion
To things-in-themselves of no certain end,
Neither as to meaning, nor peace of mind?
Unless to strip all thought of progress from
My progress and make space for a dream,
Or backlight to a stormy day, itself
At the same work, striking like lightning a shelf
Of rock where sea-birds splinter into flight
As once again I make it in by night,
Only this time somehow a different person
Dead on my feet but my mind wide open
In the wake of the day, still arriving, long after
Arrival at somewhere still yet farther
Off – neither ahead nor behind mean time
In a state of mind that works like a dram
That slowly turns the hour half-seas over
As glasses drown on the bar counter
And hands reach out in time to save them.

Broadband is down, they say. We tilt abeam,
Careening, cut off from the world . . .
Now Tigh na Mara's guests lie foetus-curled –
The elderly ladies, the two bikers, and I –
Make the night-crossing back towards day
Dreaming a silver lining to the morning.
Dreaming of Mrs MacLean's black pudding.
'The making of it,' she said, meaning the Full
Barra Breakfast I forego . . . or else I'll
Miss the 7am *Lord of the Isles*
Who made it over in spite of gales.
Out of thin air materialised just now

In a smirr of rain beyond my window.
Now water becomes land and water everywhere
Becomes South Uist. As I step ashore
Fishing parties in four-by-fours (at least
Not plus-fours) leave the hotel and head west
Careless of the day's unfolding pastoral
That brings the crofters in to Lochboisdale
To sell and talk sheep (in Gaelic): ewe lambs
And gimmers and wedders, and rams
From Frobos and Rhughasinish;
And to down a drink before they finish
Talking of this and that . . . yon Dougie Walker
Missing three days, his face on a poster.
Identifying marks: a tattooed hinge
In the crook of each arm. 'Out on a binge . . . '
'Feared drowned . . . ' So the present accumulates
Around Dougie Walker . . . and waits and waits.
I wait. There's more time to the hour here
Than you could shake a stick at and fewer
Miles. The clock flies out of the window where
Light and weather are the only measure
In the round of seasons. The tide's embrace
All there is to come and go by. The pace
Of things all dwelling and meander
As if in imitation of water.
I ride north, aboard the Post Office bus,
Via twenty-seven letterboxes
Wide-eyed-window-gazing, sole passenger
Of Morag Walker and her humour
At the work she has, her twenty-seven keys,
Her haul a small one on the best of days.
At Iochdar Junction comes Archie Campbell
And the talk meanders as we travel
To another Northwest Frontier. 'Dreadful,
Dreadful place,' says Morag. 'That shithole,'
Urges Archie, whose sons have fought there,
One due another tour in October.
As is my son . . . We share a look and wish
Them safe return come spring to Balivanich,
The airport where his youngest Domhnall
Phadruig landed last, proud of his medal:
The Conspicuous Gallantry Cross for
Dicing with death, to build a bridge, under fire

In that 'Dreadful, dreadful place.' 'That shithole . . . '
Who can enlist to celebrate the soul
While others die in such a cause or Game?
Some thought I recall of Sorley MacLean.
Right or wrong. My course is set for Raasay,
The long way round. Tonight, Lochmaddie.
And here they are, the shooting party
Up from Hertfordshire – and suddenly
I'm MacNeice across the Minch of time
But upside down (and less adept at rhyme) –
A syndicate of builders bantering,
Waiting on their ghillie, reckoning
Their tally so far: a hundred greylag,
Four hundred golden plover . . . in the bag,
In the name of the island's economy.
Lost for words, I read in my pocket anthology
Highlands & Islands: Poetry of Place
Lines from Duncan Ban MacIntyre's 'In Praise
Of Ben Dorain' where deer and man
Become each other, lead each other on,
Body and soul in nature's mortal dance
Of being-in-the-world, beyond romance.
Romance the serpent in paradise,
Our folly ever to idealise.
'Art itself must have begun as nature'
Where the seen is rooted in matter . . .
Says a piece in the *island news & ADVERTISER*
Where I find what holds the world together
('Comann na mara' Society of the Sea):
The Greylag Goose Management Committee;
Bagpipe Music at the College of Piping . . .
To say nothing of texting and Skyping,
Hands across the sea, *O trompe l'oeil.*
So near, so far, again to say goodbye.
Now I've salt on my cheek and a rheumy
Northeasterly eye, as we make for Skye
On a stiff crossing. There's spray on my lens.
So time's filtering of memory begins.

Now as agile as fingers on a chanter,
Keep note and let go. Forget to remember.
Remember to forget. Gulls keen and blaze
Beyond a dark night's window. I gaze

Through the shadows back into my head.
The crew ditch more fish-waste. The fire's fed
And Port Righ harbour's incandescent
Like a lighthouse lamp at some distant
Seamark. I lie in the dark and listen
To the ravenous din, as far back as I can,
Into my own wake, drowning in sleep,
Somewhere beyond the sea, right off the map . . .
Until woken by my notebook banging to the floor.
Now today stirs, soon to head for Sconser,
To catch the morning ferry Raasay-bound,
Its tense the future leaping like a hind.
Though *Loch Striven*, with no spring in her step,
Leaves elegance to the waves. See them leap
And bound at her shoulders, her raised car ramp,
Her short scut tracing an arc like chalk on damp
Slate this bleak grey morning of gusts and rain.
The Cuillins shape-shift, shadow and outline:
If Raasay didn't exist they'd have had to invent her
Just to be seen from Suishnish to Eyre,
Clachan to Fearns on the high hill road
But she has no need of any other world.
Inner or outer, self or other? Neither,
But one seamless presence, true to nature,
Green and sere and ripe now as the rowan,
Bejewelled with berries, about to spawn
Like a fish with eggs in golden gravel,
In Inverarish Burn, above a plunging pool.

I did not come by open boat to Raasay House
To walk the lawn and talk of other days;
But to see what the moment might discover.
'The skipper thinks he has seen you before,'
Says the ticket man. Am I from Greenock?
A man from HQ? Spying for Cal-Mac,
Making a promotion film towards a sell-off?
I laugh and wave goodbye. The sea runs rough.
The schoolchildren hurry from the bus
For the last sailing home. I try to guess
Their lives down the guttering winter days
To the year's turning and wilder seas.
Tomorrow I'll be back to guess again
But bound for Hallaig Wood in sun and rain

My route-march, solitary pilgrimage,
By wood and ridge to pay time homage.

I came there driven by more than passion
As far as North Fearns, by one Euan.
We talked of old feuds and sheep. Though my thoughts
Were of girls, coming and going, their ghosts
Metamorphosed into saplings. Until
On the verge below, as we ran downhill,
I saw a black woman like someone spectral
Out of Empire. Swaddled in her shawl,
A white infant. 'How are you?' Euan asked.
'Cold!... what do *you* think?' she laughed.
So far from Kenya, some TV wildlife
Presenter's nanny, sampling the wild life.
So times change and yet Raasay stands still,
Here above Inner Sound, and round the hill,
Below Beann na Leac, the plashy green way
To the poet's cairn, trig point to my day.

Art itself must have begun as nature.
Come in here. Take time. Take shelter.
Wait with only the wren for company
Under the green and dripping canopy.
Stand still. Gaze patiently. Acclimatise.
Absorb the world itself before your eyes.
Feel the weight of history on her knees:
The foursquare ruin, the silver-birch trees
All past child-bearing. And hidden somewhere,
Stock still with timeless stare, the deer.
Not outer but inner turned inside out,
Evicted, cleared into a green thought
As poignant as ever the poet dreamed
Of those girls. But now time the ferry claimed
Me away to the road, where the long climb
To Clachan rose, as if to kingdom come.
And on the tenth day I came down to Sleat
To Sabhal Mòr Ostaig where the elite
Stare down all English speech in stiff silence,
In age-old *ressentiment*'s deep grievance.
Higher above them, gazing out, not down,
Marxist, soldier, poet: Sorley MacLean.
What pressure on them, what future for their cause?

My privilege to hear their native noise.
What will happen? I sit and say nothing,
Inward at Ostaig. I think of running
Out a line in Welsh. But who'd understand?
So what will happen? I mean in Scotland
At fate's ballot box. Will heart or head decide?
Wear your heart on your sleeve. There is a tide,
You know, once taken will change history.
But God spare us your kilted-Tory monarchy.
Up the Republic! I say, heart on sleeve,
And praise the world for which I grieve.

Ten days on the road, as many weeks here
On the page. What better yield per hour
But to what end? That old thing-in-itself
Or something out beyond, in daily life?
Not either/or – but both? An 'I' speaking
To 'you' inspiring action from meaning?
It's not my call. Mine only to move on,
Zoom in and out, enjoy my delusion,
At the heart of recall, as the satellite
Picture shows what the weather's like tonight
Across the Minch or out in Barra Sound,
In Hallaig Wood – my far-cry fishing ground,
My evermore and my *arrière-pays* –
My loss, it seems, deep-rooted in my DNA
Of which what's not Celtic is Norse Viking,
According to Professor Sykes. So scraping
My inner cheeks to help my sister know
Her paternal line gave me a glow . . .
Pulled me up short, to find my fate brought home –
Not by ferry or foot, but Y-chromosome –
To ponder strange facts, as if by sixth sense:
Instinct and conduct explained by science?
My descent's direct from 'The Tribe of Oisin'
With only a Viking or two in-between.
What does it mean? Answers on a postcard,
Photos of islands north-northwest preferred.
Meanwhile, my video software installed,
I replay my voyage, my hard disk filled
With the poetry of departure and arrival
To keep me on course and an even keel
As November closes down and winter

Raids in its wake, storming the harbour,
And with its aftermath of winnowed light
Redeems the moment and redeems the heart.
What is this solace we all crave, the loss
That cannot speak its name? No Paradise
On Earth. No Heaven. No Good Society
But that rode roughshod over some body
Of 'others' time and truth will bring to light
And in whose cause again stand up and fight.
Yet still we must hold fast and try to keep
Our heads above water – however steep,
However high it climbs, by peak and trough,
To drag us down – we must keep faith
In something like an island community
That knows the spring will come, and the ferry.

Lighthouse at Daybreak

The coast clamoured at sea all night,
The island a meteor with a short wake
Flashing, warning and greeting.
Now come ashore, everywhere, as the early riser
The early tide, shoals to the gunwales.
Dear hearts and poor hearts blessed
Or bereaved, berthing and birthing
In the old round, find everything new today:
Waders in the surf-mouth wheeling
Jumble of weed and waste, trial and error,
What pays the rent and shapes the hour.

Nightwatch

On the lonely back road when the stars were rising
Above the island and the ocean's nightwatch began
I passed myself coming back without a word between us
And not so much as a look from him of greeting
Though there was light enough to be seen.
How I remembered the world had once been
Beyond words and the day's mysterious business
Too vast and teeming to contend with for a moment.
My need shames me now for my blather
Who'd kept to himself so well all shades of thought
And dumb appetite for days hardly speaking.

Critique of Judgement

And suddenly the view looks as though
An artist has been busy with her pastels,
Blunting the mountains and the hills
With mist of cloud and blue-green shadow:

Things for which god knows I'm a soft touch
No matter I can see through the gauze
To Nature red in teeth and claws
And hardship far beyond her crayon's reach.

This is what I call visionary appearance
To save me from the worst when I most need it
As when at any hour of day or night
I wake before pure reason's incoherence.

On Looking into an Old Photograph

How being here leads home –
Never more heartfelt, the garden
And house seeming out of reach
Deep inland. *Here*, I protest again –
But drift north-northwest in mind
To a close horizon I might touch
With sea-light in the sky above
That promising unpromised land.

Will I ever see you again, my love?
I ask quietly in monochrome,
As I steer between travel deferred
And the pleasure of deferral,
Changing down to first from third,
To all but a halt on time's hill.

An English Airman's Death Recalled
Words for Sound and Voices...

i.m. Flight Sergeant Alfred Tizzard (1915–1941), born West Preston (Littlehampton), West Sussex; buried Cillmhuirbhigh, Árainn

Scene 1

Darkness audible. Flurrying air. Distant noise of plane droning, spluttering, spiralling with a roar and flame into the drink. Broken voices on intercom: 'May-Day, May-Day...' Silence. Sound of wind and sea. Time passes. Then hiss of rope and net-hauling followed faintly by voices in Irish — snatches against sea-sound and rowing and headway.

ALFRED:
Three fishermen hauled me up in their nets. I spilled
inboard with the catch. Little left to keep my corpse
together, all slime and slither to the touch. It was spring
... That much I remember.

FIRST IRISH VOICE (*muted murmur gradually emerging*):
*Seo, féach ar na páipéirí atá air. An bhfuil tú in ann déanamh
amach cén t-ainm atá air?* [Here, look at the papers that are
on him. Can you make out his name?] (*Fade.*)

ALFRED:
But where I was I didn't know. I heard them talking over
their oars against the waves. I heard them faintly...

SECOND IRISH VOICE (*murmur gradually emerging*):
Ceapaim go n'iarann sé AL-FRED TIZZ-ARD... An fear bocht
... [I think it says Al-fred Tizz-ard ... Poor man ...]
(*Fade.*)

ALFRED:
I could not make out a word.

THIRD IRISH VOICE (*muted murmur gradually emerging*):
*Tabharfaidh muid adhlacadh glan dhó in ainm dílis Dé. Céard
eile is féidir linn a dhéanamh ach sin?* [We'll give him a clean
burial by the grace of God. What more can we do than
that?] (*Fade.*)

ALFRED:
And here they managed my remains, laid me to rest
under this far wall, just inside their sacred ground. A
sweet place. Not sour graveyard clay but limestone light
as air.

*Sound of waves breaking in long drawn-out rush and boom and retreat, and
again ... Terns shrieking shrilly. Waders piping and whirring all a-chatter.
Lark ascending windborne. Faintly and intermittently the distant crex-crex of
a corncrake. Call of cuckoo. A light blustering wind in dune grass and droning
in telephone wire. Trit-trot of hoofbeats approaching and disappearing through
the warp of sound.*

Many might hope when their number's up for such a
resting place ... in such a graveyard by the sea.

*Waves breaking ... Waders calling ... Trit-trot of hoofbeats ... Crex-crex of
corncrake ...*

STRANGER:
I'd put my name down for it if I could, stare at the stars
in sound of the sea and wading birds and horses' hooves
... to eternity.

ALFRED:
Do you know, I saw my parents here one day, Cecil and
Emily, in the flesh, come to bring me home. They talked
in dumbshow pathos: mother in tears, father upright. Or
were they Pathé ghosts, troubled spirits to my own
caught up in hurtling newsreel, dumbshow from *The
Battle of the Atlantic* screened against a bed-sheet in the
village hall? ...

CECIL TIZZARD (*aside*):
We had our own war too. That spring of '41 the German
planes bound for Portsmouth bombed us night after
night, their Heinkels thundering overhead ... Once we
saw a German airman fall to earth in broad day. A flying-
boot came off as he fell and flew away. And after it, his
pocket-watch dropped invisibly, later found still ticking
like a bomb in someone's garden, a 17-jewel 'Aero
Neuchatel'.

EMILY TIZZARD:
The things you remember...

STRANGER:
...And forget. The work of exhilarated being in
memory's forge, drama and grief seared into us.

ALFRED:
Charmed by the sweetness of the place, they chose to
leave me where I was among the good people who
brought me ashore here in the 'West'.

STRANGER:
Many there were still in those days would never lift a
body from the waves for fear the sea would take revenge
on them one day.

ALFRED:
I would have preferred to have gone home. I would have
preferred my three score years and ten lived out in
Littlehampton on Arun's shore, not Aran.

STRANGER:
A vowel shift from last to first... Brythonic to Gaelic,
changed up in one to climb *uoiea*... Twin-Wasps at
highest pitch heavenward.

ALFRED:
I would have preferred oblivion. But what will be will be
and here I haunt as I was born a stone's throw from the
sea...

IRISH VOICES (together and singly, incantatory):
We were those fishermen: Brian Peter Stephen Hernon,
Tom Feeney Hernon, Bartley Feeney Hernon. We rest
on our oars here now, all but forgotten beyond name.

STRANGER (*aside*):
Here then, I throw you lifelines. I knew you all, my
neighbours once. Brian and his pints of craic, his horse
day-long in its shafts weary of waiting and thirst outside
the pub. (Its forerunner buried on the strand below,

Father Behan presiding.) Bartley they called 'The Yank'
back from America fond of a newspaper. His brother
Tom the one I rowed with to the Callagh. We too should
have drowned that night but it wasn't our time. Although
fate fingered the third of us, marked him for another
hour. 'Lost at sea' his stone says here together with *The
Lively Lady*.

*Wind picks up. Voice of Shipping Forecast predicting gales rising to Storm 10
in sea areas Shannon, Malin ... visibility poor ... High wind- and sea-roar.
Now faintly:*

BRIAN HERNON:
I asked no priest's permission. I dug his grave and gave
him a decent burial, poor man, under a home-made cross.
A Protestant he turned out. Father Killeen never forgave
it. A right bastard, that one ...

COLEY GILL, shipwright:
I made the cross. My sister nursing for the British Army
by chance knew Alfred's sister. Small world, you say, and
life is short. No man can be living forever. We have a
saying here, you know: *Is ioma ní is buaine ná an duine ...*
[There's many a thing more lasting than a person ...]
And war the worst. We saw it here, the battleships close
to shore, the planes roaring low the length and breadth of
the island, the bodies ... The sea is nowhere neutral. It
knows no nation or peace. But the timber and other
salvage from the convoys were a boon to us for sure.

STRANGER (*aside*)
Many's the body they left at the tide-mark, I'm told.
What were they to do with so many perished airmen and
seamen?

*Storm gradually subsides. Softer snatches of sea-sound, wave-break, windborne,
sound-warp as earlier. Alfred now distractedly, as lost in thought:*

ALFRED:
Stranger, I remember you in your time. I used to watch
you come and go ... how long ago? ... How old are you?
... Had I lived I would be 97 now.

Sea-sound, wave-break, windborne, sound-warp penetrated by noise of a light aircraft on a wide circuit overhead.

> What news have you brought me, what rest might I find at last?

Plane passes noisily low overhead. Aside:

> I swear they do that to torment me. Curse the day Aer Arann was invented . . .

Noise merges into steadier throb as of seaplane and machine-gun fire as from a Focke-Wulf Condor, with voices: 'Do you copy?' 'Roger . . . ' 'May-Day, May-Day . . . ' et cetera. Alfred's voice fading:

> I remember . . .

STRANGER:
> Tell me . . .

ALFRED:
> Nothing . . .

Scene 2

MoD RECORDS OFFICER (*clipped English, businesslike*):
> Here is what we know. Here's what the records show. (*Clears throat.*) Here are the facts. Alfred's Catalina left Oban about a quarter to six on Saturday evening, the 19th of April (Lieutenant Breese, Warrant Officer Bond, Sergeant McRae aboard . . .)

STRANGER (*distractedly*):
> But what can facts do, after the fact – so long ago . . . ?

ALFRED:
> A makeshift crew. Not all of us had flown together before . . . Young Breese . . . I remember. Doomed youth. A boy, he seemed to me, being as I was all of twenty-six myself.

MoD RECORDS OFFICER:
> Flight Lieutenant Henry Francis Dempster Breese, age

twenty-two . . . Son of Air Vice-Marshall Charles Demp-
ster Breese . . . of Knightsbridge. Father also fell, the
month before: 5th March 1941, a prang in transit in the
North of Scotland.

ALFRED (*distractedly*):
Cliff Bond, Alex McRae . . .

MoD RECORDS OFFICER:
Left for Loch Erne that night, alighting at ten to eight
and leaving at a quarter past nine down the Donegal
Corridor to escort a convoy. There would have been ten
aboard her. Not all were named in the record.

STRANGER:
No ink to spare their going . . .

MoD RECORDS OFFICER:
In those early days, they died like flies . . .

ALFRED (*distractedly*):
Failed . . . I failed, heart-failed falling . . . In the dumb
cold depths. Into the mesh like a fish, swept . . . A safety-
net against 'Lost at sea'. But I never fail to return. I . . . fail
only in returning, turning and returning, condemned . . .
like a soul damned.

STRANGER:
Such is the work of war on the mind of soldier, parent,
sister, brother, wife, child . . . peasant in field, tormented
brigadier . . . broken family, heartbroken forever and ever
as in the Lord's Prayer without the amen.

Background sound of Aer Arann plane circuiting . . .

ALFRED:
But tell me, tell me more . . . If facts are all you have, let
facts do for me.

MoD RECORDS OFFICER (*intermittent background noise of plane*):
On Sunday 20 April . . . at half-past eight at night a
Sunderland Short (Flight Lieutenant Aikman, Pilot
Officer Coutts, Pilot Officer Chapman) left to search for
you and your comrades.

43

ALFRED (*distractedly*):
The Sunderland Short ... The best for me, that old
boneshaker Pegasus, so light in alighting. You know what
you can do with your Catalina ... Nothing so well.

MoD RECORDS OFFICER (*intermittent background noise of plane*):
Approaching half-past nine a message from Stranraer
gave a bearing for you. At twenty past midnight on the
21st the rear gunner sighted flares in the starboard
quarter.

ALFRED (*distractedly*):
I saw only stars port or starboard. Fleeting flare-like,
tear-like at the corners of my eyes as I fell.

MoD RECORDS OFFICER (*intermittent background noise of
seaplane*):
They searched the area, dropping flares by parachute ...
but neither sight nor sign until at twenty past one a weak
signal suggested some had made it to a life-raft. They
combed the dark acres of ocean tirelessly. Dead reck-
oning their name for it, quartering blind, hour on end.
Another hour and they set course for Eagle Island to
recheck their position. They searched until, at nearly ten
to five that April morning as sleep on earth turned its last
corner, they were above Slyne Head, nine miles south-
west of Clifden in Co. Galway. And they went on
searching until just gone half past eight, when they called
it a night and headed for base and breakfast. And so it is
now on the RAF headstone Alfred's date of death is
given 21st April 1941, age 26. But how long he was in the
sea we do not know.

... Ten minutes on ...

*(Words broken intermittently by background noise of machine-gun fire and roar
of planes):*

... and they came under attack. But it broke off at 1000
yards without hitting and they were waterborne at
Lough Erne by quarter past ten, lucky to be living. After-
noon saw them in Oban, dog-tired making for their
billets, at the Great Western or the Esplanade, the

Alexandra or the Marine. Those are the facts of all we know... None survived. All, bar Alfred, lost at sea, or somewhere in an unmarked grave. We do not know.

STRANGER:
But what can telling such a story do? For whom? Harrowing instruction, respite in reverence, therapy in reminding, belated atoning. The pity whose and going where? For whom to read or care? Those who wield world-power and thrive through trouble and denial, evermore wired for wisdom in hindsight... ?

ALFRED (*growing fainter...*):
And is that what brought you here?

STRANGER:
No, I came for your memory, to know what might be known and write it down. And for myself, it is true, for solace and reflection, to make good my losses, where I once lived true... as never again, as true as living gets. For doom too, the life ahead... It seems... For I have a son, older than you were then, off to Afghanistan this coming autumn. A waste of breath... the years behind. It seems... (voice breaking up) History put to flight... The facts ignored.

Sound of plane coming nearer and mounting crescendo of noise of WW2 warfare growing into modern warfare.

ALFRED (*faintly*):
Speak up... I... can't... hear. I...

Enormous explosion ... dying slowly into nearing then fading sound of Aer Arann plane and gradual return of waves breaking in long drawn-out rush and boom and retreat, and again ... Terns shrieking shrilly. Waders piping and whirring all a-chatter. Lark ascending windborne. Faintly and intermittently the distant crex-crex of a corncrake. Call of cuckoo. A light blustering wind in dune grass and droning in telephone wire. Trit-trot of hoofbeats approaching and disappearing through the warp of sound.

Finis

'The sea goes all the way round the island'

For they were long days, though short,
And short nights, though winter-long,
Rising before day into the deep thought
That is being, undistracted, like a song
In its tune, seamlessly one and the same.
As the man said: the sea goes all the way
Round the island. But here too like a half-rhyme,
Holm and home, headway and tideway,
Between compass-point and landmark
Asymmetric revelation does its work
And rounds the mind for another day.

On the Rocks Road

There . . .

Preserve us I say
From narrow-gauge minds
But not narrow roads
With green spines
Where the heart's affections
Put best foot forward:
Between two stone walls
Built to the rhythm
Of rock-form and contour
Of labour and time
Straight as a die
Dipping in and out of sight
Opening and narrowing
Ahead behind – behind ahead
In threadbare karst country
Grown where nothing grows
Better than light and lichen
Rare alpine, common thorn,
Atlantic gale and storm
Limestone, stone by stone
Advancing to delay
To the last angle and oval
With makeshift-erratic
Punctuation of granite –
As now at home recalling
I step up from Cill Rónáin
Over the top and down
To Gort na gCapall
(a.k.a. West Cork)
The field of the horse
On my solitary walk
Unpicking as I go
The old formula:
Distance over speed and time –
Beyond recognition
In my mind-body economy
Of presences and memory
In and out of step

Balancing line on line
Not carelessly picked
Or casually piled
But as those men worked
With steady eye and hand.

But hold your step
As the Rocks Road
Has ever done
Since it began
Never to travel its own length
Nor time its progress
Never to see but to be
From end to end
Its centre of gravity where
But here and there?
In infinite recession
Beyond the sum of knowledge
Beyond botany book
And guide to birds
Studies of fossils
Or place-names
In the folds of a map
And where the wild rose
Blows in nothing's name.
What do I bring?
Nothing it knows.
What do I take?
Nothing it will miss.
Where am I bound?
To the field of the horse.

And back . . .

As now I am again
Stepping out of time
Working my way in
From the port
Of the fort's mouth
Through a giant jetsam
Of rock and boulder
Beside which sea-wall

The village of the horse takes shelter
Itself an island in a sea of stone
Safe as houses but no safer
As a FOR SALE sign tells
Wired to a garden gate
The rogee Time at work
Waiting on the highest bidder
No safer than mortality:
The O'Flaherty home
Of radical fame.
A story to be told there
But to the stranger more
One of stage directions
With pauses and no text between
Where no one seems to live
But when the little bus comes round
A woman disembarks
With shopping bags from 'SUPERMAC'S'
To disappear indoors
And at evening an old man
Emerges to Flymo the lawn
And two brothers further on
Look up startled as
I take them by surprise
Calling as I go: 'Fine evening!'
And at once bend back
To hack at briars
As if lifetimes ago
Drifting into silence behind me
In deepening shadow
As the day fades
And evening sharpens
To monochrome
Then dims to a glimmer of lights
Beside the sea's fire
And the nightwatch begins
Behind drawn curtains
Via dish and aerial
As I start the steep climb
Back the way I came
Out of sight out of mind
Out of mind into vision
And I pass myself

Coming back in silence
The way not the same
My step different
Though not my passion
For the Rocks Road.
Do not ask life's purpose
But live every step of the road
(The time it takes knows
Nothing of distance or speed)
In the world of matter
And mind brought together
As in making's invention
I write this for you:
Call it ordinariness
Call it best of all love
As the walls ahead touch
At their vanishing point
And keep opening.

Cormorant

The sea's too big for the cormorant's digestion,
Yet it grabs it in its beak, flashing and scaled.
Baptism by fire its routine, then total immersion.
On neither count has it so far failed
The old argument from experience to resurrection.

Remember, nothing in Nature but man is cursed.
And take heart for every day truth stands revealed
Beyond the beholder, as long as life might last,
Glinting like a weather-vane above the Seamen's Mission,
A starry riding-light atop a pitching mast.

Port Sheánia Revisited

The hooded crows work on ahead
Combing the tidemark in no-man's-land.
Wind flutters their brief flights to avoid me.
So places travel on the spot to and fro
And round and away in the heart's wake.
The cormorants hang out on table rock
As ever at low tide, drying their wings,
Digesting both species of pollack and
Squirting out a gouache of honeyed shit.
Curlew and oystercatcher compare notes
On a scale of limpidity beyond reckoning.
Two eggs in a tern-scrape of pebble and shell
Have become three since yesterday.
No one comes here any more to disturb them,
To harvest sea-candles or periwinkles
Nor an armful of driftwood for the fire.
This goes on all day, all night, without human agency.
Why should that not console me?

Harbour Inn

The sea wants for nothing yet is all lack . . .
What enchants me here I chant
To its hunger, its drunken slap and smack,
Its chain-link rattle, as the day's slant
Grey goes reeling, with highlight
Of gannet, gull, and white-horse mane,
Rain on stone, on slate, and skylight,
Out there beyond the window-pane

Where the ferry's making heavy weather
As if caught mid-Sound in a painting.
See how it wallows, treading water.
Who knows whether it's coming or going?
Surely the folk in here know
Who as to souls in peril and distress
Keep one eye on the clock's slow
Hands, the other on their glass.

On Not Sailing to St Kilda

The windows shut against the weather,
I climbed the hill through bog and heather.

I saw a golden eagle and a mountain hare
And found an antler of a deer.

I walked along Hushinish shore
And watched the gannet plunge down ice-cold air.

All in a southeast wind I saw forever
Nothing to my mind that might repair

The dream of sailing to St Kilda
As I had dreamt it months before.

A Return of the Native

And this comes to its end, not to be met with again,
Though weather and season make the best match they can
Tuning wind and rain to the hour and the storm-lit dawn.
And not everyone has passed on and some return
But time has taken them and what they were is gone
Into the depths of heart and mind towards oblivion
But for love's last hold on her companion reason
Sustained by epiphanies on hope's frugal pension,
Never in sharper relief what cannot now be done or undone.

Blind

After the eye of the storm:
The eye of the net-mender's needle.

Working as at Ithaca
On the quay to all mythologies

And bloody reckoning
In the mind's gaping.

The monofilament spool
Unwinding and weaving in and out

The timeless yarn of the blind:
Not a line but a net of lines.

Consigning oblivion to oblivion
In the play of work.

Requiem

Dress his days to a dextrous and starlight order.

Gerard Manley Hopkins

1

Night blooms shadows among clouds like damaged lungs.
The carry-outs are busy and spring is in the offing.
Men in half-lit wheelhouses prepare for the night's fishing.
Smokers hang in doorways bleakly staring, cold, hooked on
                                            last-gasp cigs
Like conscripts about to go over the top to certain death,
Or disaffected sentries. The Esplanade imagines things in
                                            monochrome
With patrician soundtrack from Pathé, or footage from *Atlantic Convoy.*
In the cockpit of my top-floor hotel room I stare at my instrument
                                            panel:
Paper, pen and ink – and dream my next sortie. No dead reckonings
On the muse's missions, just the waste of waters and the hit or miss
Of chance, abandonment more in the spirit of that Irish airman
Than anything anyone in the squadron entertained
Though some on foot, like Douglas, knew what the poet intended.
So-and-so had a 'good war' (discuss). A war by any other name . . .
Many strange meetings. The other night after dinner
The Brigadier sat next to me wept as the port went round.
I saw him with my own eyes in the blur of subdued light.
He kept on talking while the tears ran down his high-boned cheeks.
It might have been a scene at Craiglockhart long ago.
'We have yet to understand what "collateral" means for this
                                            generation,'
One remarked next day as to PTSD; and I had already seen,
Startling awake, struggling for air, my son stood over me,
The night before, a foot taller than he is wherever he is 'semi-feral . . .'
'On a recce call-sign' by Helmand River. Six weeks and not a word.
Neither love nor fear can tolerate a vacuum. But how soft we are
Compared with then. I mean the *durée* in 'the duration'.
So many silences at the heart of battle resounding as if to eternity.
('We will remember them.') The reach of suffering lost in action
As invasive as water by the Somme.
Then the knock at the door and the shadow beyond it.

It was evening. The garden sodden with winter, hawthorn's stark
crown
Against the last of a December day. I came in and opened my
inbox, idly,
On the *qui vive* and there found at last my 'Field (Service) Post Card'
Slipped in on the ether under cover like a star into a dark night.
'Our early weeks there were dominated by close-quarter
engagements.'
A thrill of armchair courage and pride like the curse of a general's
strategy,
A politician's lie (imperious white lie), ran through my veins,
Or was it mere relief made the hair on the back of my neck stand
To hurried attention, as if late on parade? Then the thought came to me.
Free verse is war epitomised: strict drill, routines blown apart
Revealing fault-lines, fracturing up the chain of command
Where the sergeant-major struts up and down before a parade of
ghosts.
Hear him barking pentameters and dactyls, bristling
Like a demented German shepherd, his masters whistling for him
In the European dark, joint winners of the Nobel Prize for Peace.
Insurgent or fanatic, military success but political failure, victory or
Defeat. Tick the boxes according to preference, you 'pernicious race
Of little odious vermin' as the general's horse whinnied under his
breath
Prancing on the parade ground, clopping, jingling, his nibs
In full ceremonial jackboots and cuirass, the works, muttering
Honi soit qui mal y pense, a grenadier whistling snatches from '*Lillibulero*'.
Pomp and circumstance. Hearts and minds. Tell it to: 'The
likely INS,
The spies, the elderly one-time mujahadin'. Tell it to: 'The
barefoot girl
No older than seven walking her cow through icy fields'.
Tell it to the marines that their fallen comrades did not die in vain.
Tell it to the hardy Helmundi Pashtuns who saw off the Russians
And now the airhead Romans of the western empire, empty-handed
Back where they came from, their cover stories already ghosted for
them.
Tell it to the poppy fields, and the opiate of Remembrance Day.
Tell it any way you like but know little humanity touches is true
quite.

I stood with the townspeople, observed the silence, the laying of
                                                    wreaths,
By the various causes and worthies, the WI, the local Masonic Lodge,
Heard the last post and watched their faces, solemn, respectful,
Trying to imagine my own among them, one of many –
More than ever, in recent memory, they said – but distracted in thought
By the earlier talk of men near me, one or two campaign medals apiece,
On faded ribbons, and younger men with more, perhaps for bravery,
And this old falangist of Queen and Country, retired from the Met,
Speaking of Sovereignty and Treachery and the 'Heart of England',
His 'group' at work studying Constitutional Law with a view to
                                                    bringing
Charges of treason against Blair and Cameron on the question of
                                                    Europe.
And the others listening inscrutably, without dissent, staring at
                                                    their feet,
Not a hint of a smile or disbelief, their worlds their remembrance what?
Elsewhere in the crowd how many thinking of their own flesh and blood
In harm's way as winter bites into Helmand and farmers harvest at last,
Crops to them, cover to the fighters, and in each feuding village
Rival calls to prayer resound along the river and if you close your ears
The countryside but for its compounds and the cold might be
                                                    somewhere
In rural Kent or Suffolk at the height of autumn, but for the
                                                    seven-year-old
Circling round on a motorbike with five- and three-year-old siblings
On the pillion, but for the patrols, the air strikes, the horror worse
                                                    than fear.
And the roll call of lives claimed with nothing to say of what's in a name.
And the policy pronouncements a paper trail beyond oblivion
Come out of nowhere like a sudden enemy, a thief in the night of reason.
And when I woke up in the morning like one who made it back
From a night-sortie, combing the waves for a flare, for a signal
At the edge of sound, billeted at the Great Western or the Esplanade,
The Alexandra or the Marine, nothing was any the clearer
But the cold air as I drew up the sash window ran clean through me
And I was as if not there … the ink now dry and 'permanent' in my
                                                    name.

Insomnia

Insomniac, the night itself, out there for company,
Where tanker constellations ride in the bay:
Waiting for the price of crude to rise, waiting
For the pilot, lit up like Christmas trees,
A beauty not their own but the gazer's longing.
Someone out there keeping watch like me
Looks ashore at the ribbons of street lights,
The dock's fire of arc-lamps, over the hill,
A ghost of hotel fronts and flash of tidemark,
Waiting for the trader to call. While the night
Revels home to urban music on a beer-can,
Shark-violence kicking-off down backstreets.

The country nearby of deeper shadow folds
Into itself and sleeps through mere flotsam
In starry thistle field and hedgerow,
On moorland and hill, time out of mind –
Oblivious as the BBC goes 'Sailing By . . .'
And wide-awake I lie, listening in the dark
To the World Service, with its breezy talk,
And bad news, abroad where the lost tune-in
To paper-thin word from imperial London
And the world goes on warring, blundering,
Cavorting out of control like the sea
Beyond hearing in the pounding surf.

Round About a Great Estate

Eat your heart out in cavernous envy
Capability. Fold up the Estate map and put away
The plantation, the marsh, the bridleway,
The shooting box, the loch, the little jetty,
The fish-trap chevrons down the estuary –
Likenesses lost in divine disarray, the key
Locked on the old order and authority,
The cult of breeding and its ascendancy.
The PRIVATE keep-out and man-trap tyranny
Of that *ancien régime* of cut-glass barbarity.
The photographs of staff and tenantry,
Their story in Sunday-best for posterity
Recycled now as heritage and legacy:
The guns with their bag, keeper and ghillie,
Stalker and stag, the whisky distillery,
Captain of cavalry, captain of industry –
The whole shooting match and gallimaufry:
A seat in the House, a seat in the country,
Every conceivable cliché and hierarchy
Shored up by portfolios of gilts and property.
Blow to the four corners your *grandeur* and *folie*
Careers in Whitehall, careers at the Embassy.
Blow too what passes for your mind: the sea
Mocks in its rock garden, mocks the gently
Falling landscapes that border so privately
Their framed view, crying out to beauty,
The seven-sided sea, with its sails full of sky.
Hear the wintry roar of its eternal battery.
Observe its genius for blunt-sheared topiary
And closest nail-scissor trim in sandy
Border, and marvel you ever had your day
Between home and far-flung colony.
Put off your self. Walk the margin of the bay,
O heir to the ruin of all you survey.

Shore Leave

Turn your back on it and walk away
Until the sea's a distant memory only
Woken by inland gulls and the tidal
Rush of a motorway's perpetual
Arrival-and-withdrawal, windborne
For miles to break about town
And village, islanded farmstead,
Distant parish church with its dead
Run aground below, under headstone
After headstone in the short tide,
Poppy-wreath adrift beneath the memorial.

At the Landfill Site

I lose my way in fortune
Between the epic and everyday:
My voyage and little history
Like the swan in the street
The albatross on deck
Out of their element:
The fox at the landfill site,
Gulls set alight
Over bonfire seas of garbage.

I was turned back at the gate
Directed to an entry down the road
Reserved for books and manuscripts.
It seemed I drove for many years.
Waste management was ever
The work of third parties.
And nothing's true and nothing sacred
But what they happen to recycle.
I pulled in off the road and slept.

Once I turned and saw a ghost
Behind me on a lakeside road.
Now I startled at seeing him again.
'The journey from darkness into darkness . . . '
His dumb lips mouthed
But then he faded.
The trucks of waste tailed back beyond
Orange lights strobing into littered thorn.
I filled my notebook with another poem.